"What a graceful and beautifully crafted book by a compassionate poet who reminds us of 'how much consolation / is needed and can't be found.' William Louis-Dreyfus's meditations on the warping passage of time that 'clothes everything in losing' are especially poignant here. 'Where, when it comes, will the lightning strike?' he eloquently muses, while still exhorting us, in his wake, to 'Be subject to the dance. / Be seasonably enthralled.'"
    —Emily Fragos, author of *Hostage: New & Selected Poems*

"The poems gathered in *Letters Written and Not Sent* ramify like the branches of a great tree offering shadow and light, connecting earth and sky, arising from as much as standing for elemental mystery. The collection begins with a conclusion: 'Just as death comes, / the truth gets said.' Where do we go from there? Alive on the page, William Louis-Dreyfus speaks to us intimately, his voice combining wit with majesty in lines exploring—until embracing—human paradox: 'There is in night no light to hide behind. / It is by day that secrets can be kept.' Uprooted in childhood, exiled from the familiar, Louis-Dreyfus discovered himself at home in the gnarled syntax of John Donne and the subtle clarities of Robert Frost, early on arriving at the tragic sense Elizabeth Bishop found when contemplating the sea: 'our knowledge is historical, flowing, and flown.' Rootedness: no wonder this poet has 'a passion for the look of trees / their fixedness / their ecstasy in rising out of ground. . . .' The poems of William Louis-Dreyfus are possessed as much by a rage for social justice as a love of beauty and a childlike joy in the play of thought and the freedom of practicing an art."
    —Phillis Levin, author of *Mr. Memory & Other Poems*

"Throughout *Letters Written and Not Sent*, a long-anticipated book, William Louis-Dreyfus grapples with far-reaching themes: life and death, god and eternity, nature and civilization, light and darkness. Louis-Dreyfus's poems flash a formal versatility and elegance. He experiments with forms such as the villanelle, triolet, pantoum, and sonnet, and deftly masters the line with a pitch perfect sense of rhythm and sound. In this jewel box of a book, Louis-Dreyfus carves out each facet of his poems: 'I kept cords of wood way beyond our needs, / and shuffled for the truth, / saved in sculpted poems.'"
    —Elise Paschen, author of *The Nightlife*

"William Louis-Dreyfus's remarkable understanding of humanity and the natural world is fully represented in this collection. Louis-Dreyfus's work reveals his belief that humans have an unshakeable connection to nature, and through that to God; all are one in the same, sharing similar gifts—and ultimate treatment. Drawn to nature, he praises it boldly throughout many of these poems, particularly in 'Adjusting.' And it is within consideration of nature that he was able to, maybe not accept, but understand death, which he resolves in 'Explanation.' His poems are honest about this, never sardonic or grimly fatalistic—as without death how could nature be? However, his work in the middle of the collection reflects a constant sorrow about those hunted and persecuted by the malicious.

The collection also reveals that Louis-Dreyfus loved the ordinary—a worm, a caesura, and most strikingly, everyday moments such as a drawer being opened. He challenges us to pay close attention to unobvious joys and obvious inequities, and to consider the immense possibility that we are all connected to each other in a most miraculous natural design."

—Ellen Rachlin, author of *Permeable Divide*

"How eerie that William Louis-Dreyfus's poems meditated on death, unswervingly, for years before his actual death in 2016. There's no self-pity in these taut meditations, but a stoicism reflected in the spare, chiseled lines. He was also haunted by secrets, by messages not delivered, knowledge lost. In 'What Einstein Said,' the dying physicist utters four final words, but in German, and overheard only by a nurse who can't understand him. In 'Suppose,' the baffled poet turns 'to what poems don't quite tell.' And 'Calling Out' ends by hearing the bleating of ewes whose lambs have been selected for slaughter, calling 'for three full days; and then the calling ends.'

There's rock-bottom integrity, a dignified modesty, and a quizzical persistent quest for meaning in this collection. It's a final bequest to the living from an intensely generous man."

—Rosanna Warren, author of *Departure: Poems*

LETTERS WRITTEN
AND NOT SENT

poems

WILLIAM LOUIS-DREYFUS

Red Hen Press | *Pasadena, CA*

Book design by Mark E. Cull

Library of Congress Cataloging-in-Publication Data
Names: Louis-Dreyfus, William, 1932–2016, author.
Title: Letters written and not sent : poems / William Louis-Dreyfus.
Description: Pasadena, CA : Red Hen Press, [2019]
Identifiers: LCCN 2018056115 | ISBN 9781597098694 (tradepaper)
Classification: LCC PS3612.O794 A6 2019 | DDC 811/.6—dc23
LC record available at https://lccn.loc.gov/2018056115

The National Endowment for the Arts, the Los Angeles County Arts Commission, the Ahmanson Foundation, the Dwight Stuart Youth Fund, the Max Factor Family Foundation, the Pasadena Tournament of Roses Foundation, the Pasadena Arts & Culture Commission and the City of Pasadena Cultural Affairs Division, the City of Los Angeles Department of Cultural Affairs, the Audrey & Sydney Irmas Charitable Foundation, the Kinder Morgan Foundation, the Allergan Foundation, the Meta & George Rosenberg Foundation, and the Riordan Foundation partially support Red Hen Press.

First Edition
Published by Red Hen Press
www.redhen.org

Acknowledgements

Grateful acknowledgement is made to the following publications, in whose pages these poems first appeared:

The Hudson Review: "After Reading a Very Good Poem," "Blood Sugar," "Explanation," "Ghost," "Love," "Pledge," "Sorrow," "What Happens"; *The New Criterion*: "Audit," "Calling Out," "What Einstein Said," "Where Are the Dead"; *Plume*: "A Variation," "Hart Crane," "My Mother Before She Died"; *The Southwest Review*: "Adjusting."

The author wishes to express his thanks to Phillis Levin for her intelligence and selflessness, Ellen Rachlin for her faith and fortitude, and Paula Deitz for her unbounded professionalism.

for Judy, Phyllis, Julia, Phoebe, and Emma

CONTENTS

LETTERS WRITTEN AND NOT SENT

WHAT HAPPENS

Just as death comes,
the truth gets said.
It is the anteroom
to all eternity.

It has a prismed tone
no one need turn to hear
and is an airy place
single like a sea.

Nothing gets said again.
No thought leads on to thought.
All sense is feeling then
and no infirmity.

Adjusting

I have a passion for the look of trees,
their fixedness,
their ecstasy in rising out of ground,
arms up in praise of heaven and below,
their random symmetry,
the light they make that brings the seasons on,
their contained thickness that accumulates
frail, feckless Time.
Where else is Time more materially revealed?

Someone I know prefers the look of fields,
and had dawn redwoods standing in his way.
He sold them to me at a bargain price,
if I would move them off his land to mine.
Their size required that their roots be pruned
for a growing season before they would be moved.
And so two years passed before they stood by me.

That was some years ago.
The redwoods grew as if in response
to the devout homage they were held in.
Their trunks amassed and lengthened to the top.
They spread the sky with their green symmetries.

I was away the night the storm arrived.
I saw the blasted tree in morning light.
Lightening had hit not the tree itself
but, next to it, an old water pipe,
bounced off into the tree,
both down and up, and shattered it
in pieces small enough to hold.

There have been storms since then, and raging light.
My trees stay fixed and helpless in their path.
Where, when it comes, will the lightning strike?
I think of those I love and then I note
that Nature, whatever happens next,
like God and Death, doesn't know my name.

GHOST

While I was living, mornings came.
I saw the children rise
as if it were their due.

Years passed.
The fruit tree spread to the upstairs window
where silence grew as well.

Things warped.
My wife was always taken by surprise
and grew a hunted look.

I kept cords of wood way beyond our needs,
and shuffled for the truth,
saved in sculpted poems.

Now I find it easily
and know them all by heart
as thoughtlessly as once
my breath came in and out.

SECRETS

It is in dark that sharper things are seen.
Bright light obscures by all its busyness.

It is by whisper truer things are told.
Words have their echo when only barely heard.

It is in stealth that heroes run their course.
And love's the way that sorrow stays like stone.

There is in night no light to hide behind.
It is by day that secrets can be kept.

January 13

The child believes the father knows
of what the entwined world is made.
How else did that growing up get done?

The father's ambushed by the child.
His heart-swing never sounds the same.
Love, like air, invades his place.

The poet thinks and sometimes finds
the true encasement of what is.

And you, like love, are simply life
in the throes of keeping its promise.

LOVE

There is a tick, I'm told,
small as a seed, its back
hard as a turtle's shell,
blind, they say, and lives
for years immobile
on the tip of a twig, until
sensing, they don't know how,
it makes an arc in the air
leaping a distance farther
than the moon may be for us
to land by the side of its mate.
It does this once, they say.

What Einstein Said

He spoke four words just before he died
heard by the nurse whose shift was ending
and who in those last days attended
the disease he sought no help to cure.
She heard him speak, but as she explained
to those eager to find a final meaning
in what had been said, she spoke
no German and did not understand.

The Father leaves and never tells us where
a final comfort lies, though he must know
if only by his blessing and goodbye.
We live ensnared by what can't be retrieved
or known, or kept, or made a refuge of,
and nothing's certain save what is departed.

Where Are the Dead

Where are the dead?
They are not among us.
Between this man and that
before the dead had died
stood air and space and weather
and hung the smell of things.
Today, on that same street
stand all the self-same things
between that man and this.

Where are the dead?
They die. They disappear.
Today, when we look up,
not anything's displaced.
No space has been reduced
though near a man has died.
No imprint stays of him
to interrupt our view.
Only the living show.

We were the dead's increase.
Not anything that's left
exists with them again.
The living think of life.
What secrets have we learned
that we can use to know
why nothing can explain
if death resembles life
and where the dead have gone?

A Variation

Why ask to know, twin and neighbor,
if, as it unwinds, the string of our lives
has resolution, lies in a direction,
why today's ache was once a noon pleasure.

The gods have no plan for us.
We are not seasons and will not be renewed.
Instead, note the pillow bloom of the cherry tree
and recall how winter brought it on.

CALLING OUT

It's early Spring. The sheep will have their young.
The flock then fills with lambs a few weeks old,
anonymous dots until each mother's call
brings each lamb back to get its feeding done.

The ewes call out, and by each mother's sound,
repeated like an echo round the field,
they and the lambs, wherever is the need,
each by their own are by that calling found.

If you keep sheep and mean to do it well,
you'll try to sell the lambs for Easter night
and get your price and give the flock its blend.

The ewes remaining in the flock don't know
their lambs are gone and keep on calling out
for three full days; and then the calling ends.

My Mother Before She Died

Felt such fears
that she called out in the night
to strangers in the house:
    "Are you there?"
                        "Are you there?"

My mother who forswore Company,
who knew that love was tied to blood
and nothing else,
my mother called out,
choked in fear to be alone.

Even though she knew
that there's no age to sorrow,
that going from severed to whole
is not the fearsome passage,
and that all particles unify.

It didn't help her in the end.
She had never surrendered before.

COMPANY

The rain makes a noise
in a silent house
that presupposes speech.
It has the comfort sound
of life of seasons past.
Afterwards, solitude regains
until, in the blind turn of things,
the rain comes back again.

PROGRESSION

I remember the sadness
surrounding my grandmother
always dressed in the black
of mourning for her husband
since she was a young mother
of two, the younger named
Dolores, my mother, who
also knew how sorrow lurks
and how much consolation
is needed and can't be found.

One Thing I Know About the Dead

In a place that needs no naming
men with guns and long steel blades
ride in trucks from village to village
chasing women and children
scrambling like hens on the dusty road
(the men were hunted yesterday).
Now a woman spreads her arms and falls
to cover her child stumbling away
from the arc of the swinging blade.
It doesn't reach the child
and swings through the mother's neck.
The child scurries to the underbrush.
The next morning the trucks come back,
and the child, run down again,
is slit through by the arc of the swinging blade.

Nothing intercepts its thrust,
no sudden dust-swirl clouds the view.
The Earth is still.
No thunderous apparition interrupts.

Sorrow

My daughter stares into her dresser drawer,
a moment's concentrated stillness
in the morning rush to school.

I see the line her face makes,
seen from the side
like a quarter-moon.

There are deeper creases coming
from strings of concentrated moments
chained in the unexpected life awaiting.

I may not see it marked,
but I see it now
and move to kiss the cheek smooth
that now doesn't need my smoothing.

She will one day pause and see the creases coming
on a face like hers stilled in a young moment
and move to kiss the cheek,
or whatever she will do.

I say now
being in nature's way
is consolation enough.
That's what I say.

TO A CHILD AFTER DARK

Scratching

        is like horses' hooves

Grunting

        is like dogs asleep

Tapping

        is a water spout

Stretching

        is eagles airing

Blinking's

        not a butterfly

Snowflakes

        put you warm in bed

Thinking

        is a winged ride

Dreaming's

        the color of singing voices

Sleeping

        makes the morning dew

Waking's

        what comes after night

Smiling

        is the morning light.

Pledge

I promise never to speak of how heavily
my father and mother weigh on me, unless
my speaking at all is already a breach.
I promise to compose in a room without mirrors
and never to use one word where none will do.
I promise not to let the idea make a puppet of the word
and not to mistake my breath for the air in the line.
I promise not to church intone,
nor be swayed by the temptress called "Poem."

After Reading a Very Good Poem

You don't chew the words
though you would like to
dismantle them each
in their soundfull order
and turn each material scrap
into your nourishment.
There arises somewhere
in your middle body
a warm tightness as if
a feast had just ended.
An exhilaration fills your breath.
Nothing so winning seems possible;
perhaps like the first thought
you will have entering heaven.

Suppose

It's not being alone that makes you lonely.
It's having no one but imperfect strangers
to talk to about it. Suppose Columbus,
coming on the wilds and feathers of the new land,
had found that in his absence he had slipped
from his Queen's memory, or suppose the astronaut,
breathless at the deep blue of the planet spied
from so high up, had witnessed Houston Central
switch to track the late show instead—would they,
needing some echo of the wonders found,
turn, like you and me, to what poems don't quite tell?

Kissing

How did kissing first get started?
Did it come just after smelling?
Was that delicate admission made
in the course of lustful snorting?
Waltzes, sighs, and soft looks followed.
No sign of caring has replaced it,
not even made by the written word.
It remains the surest signal
of the movement of the heart.

FEEDING

You have seen the hummingbird
tremble and pelicans transform
into arrows and plunge,
and the leopard prance
with the arched, surrendered
dance of the gazelle in his teeth,
and the red hawk motionless
in his wing, depending
on the wind and its warmth.
They are feeding, feeding, feeding
as they are called to do.

How We Stay Sane

How good that life is filled with tiny things,
days packed with household goods,
keys, curbs, replies, an ankle itch,
the three rings it takes to get the phone.

Lucky we are that thought and feeling stay
bystanders, stilled, while the day proceeds,
densed and hunched in its little swarm of traffic.
The night's another thing,
but there are dreams to shield us.

Prescription

If you stop too long
and then think too much
(what beyond the door
does the doorknob mean?)
confusion like a swamp
will intertwine your steps.

If you recall the threads
that tapestried your life
and saw their colors run
and how the image blurred,
you will no longer need
all your recurrent breath.

Desire the antidote
will keep the meanings clear.
Exalt the rosy cheek,
the sparrow and the bear.
Be subject to the dance.
Be seasonally enthralled.

Riddle I

True makers love the dance.
They bring me to the steps
that are my own,
but don't get taken
till muscled through by them.

When in their arms,
I seem to come and go.
It's all the twirls
of making me remain
that captivates them most.

I knew a man
who dared not love the dance
and held me only
when I was not his own.

But I was born
of those who loved the dance
and left me whole
after their music stopped.

Hart Crane

One story is he just walked off the boat
while it was moving? drifting? stopped?
in gulf or coastal waters not yet warm.
The date, I think, was earlier than spring.
No one saw him again.
Did anyone see him go?

He said the sea had a cruel floor
and wrote of voyages circled in light.
Perhaps it was an erroneous report,
and all he did was only disappear.
Who's left to ask?
Why do I need to know?

Moving Not Going

Grown from reflections in our parents' eye,
dislodged, re-nested
in Brazils not seen before
to form with creatures unlike our own,
we trail the stain of forgotten pasts
like the snail its slight bubbled slime,
blind behind it.

GREAT POETS WHEN THEY DIE

don't come to earth again
for having felt it once.

Great poets while they lived,
though strapped and numbed like us,
flew off in feeling not just their own,
took thought and sinewed it to form.

God once did that to earth
and left words out until we came.

Conclusion

My father died some days ago.
He had lived longer than most people do
and yet he left me with a lot to know.

He had black feelings, which he hid, although
many around him felt them seeping through
and kept in thinness what they sought to know.

Life's varied pricks were always the greater blow.
Unnoticed went his children's black and blue
which kept them blind to what they didn't know.

He was my guide a distant time ago
and made my world center on his view.
I had his imprint fresh on which to grow.

The aging past which seems just days ago
makes images like shards, freshly coming through,
and me a slave to what I'll never know.

My father died and didn't let me know
the words and phrases that I felt he knew
and I will have, however far I go,
ever the echoes of what I cannot know.

Unless

There is in all remembering
a surround of sorrow.
No matter the thing remembered.
Even if a joy, once recalled
it is put in a pang of yearning.
Time's a culprit.
Time, who never looks the other way,
clothes everything in losing.

Unless we are like seasons
and will repeat.

America's Not Hard to See

America's not hard to see.
Behold the lustered Maple tree
before it's cut for billboard space
and then expensively replaced
by Iacocca and Miss Liberty.

America's not hard to see.
Adore the candidate's hygienic face.
Enable him to save the race
and keep us blond, both you and me,
for Sandra Day and Miss Liberty.

Darrow, King and Joe Hill are dead,
not all killed by an American hand.
Note how we cherish the brave of the land.
See how we're stirred by the half-time band.
Isn't that why past heroes bled?

America's not hard to find.
The white and pink of an American house
enshrines John Wayne and Mickey Mouse.
And what offends an American mind
is all that's other than kin and kind.

America's not hard to be.
Gird yourself up for novelty.
Half the price for two of each,
packaging is what we teach.
Tinseled neon is what we crave.

America will be hard to save.
And whatever the echoes of the American song,
America will be hard to mourn.

To the Worm

We, thought-drenched, word-strapped rulers of the world,
temple builders, anointers of heroes and invented gods,
who amass discoveries, dogmas, machines, designs,

discern how richly the earth is made and suited
for our use in our strict and not-so-slow progress to rot,
don't draw our worship down to where you are

or notice you, who, unless you move,
no one can tell by what end you start
to take your godly action and make life's cradle.

JACKSON, MISS., NOVEMBER 6, 1987

Ross Barnett, Segregationist, Dies
—The *New York Times*

Whoever thought the earth was flat
had the advantage of having died
long before it was proved round
so not to have to change his smile,
his pose and or his argument.
Even orators who mid-speech
watch the hall just empty out
may still believe, and still be right,
it's the majority that's always wrong.

Children, I think, always expect
that grown-ups, when they come to find
their common world does not reflect
a view they separately held,
like heroes who are bound to truth
and cannot their own honour flee,
can be relied upon to use
the love they got from growing up
to stand for what they thought was wrong.

I wonder how Ross Barnett felt
for twenty years before he died
watching the world relentlessly,
and with no reference to him,
reverse in steady usefulness
the view he championed while he lived.
Oh, if I were a fool like him
and shame were not a constant threat,
I might get better verses made
or else not know it when I didn't.

The Killing of Billy Furr

—Newark Race Riot, July 1967

Perhaps it's right that Billy Furr should die,
All twenty-four years of him, in shoes his brother wore.
I'd like to point to where the shoes passed on.
And though I can't, I know of course they did.

Perhaps it's right, though shocking sad of course,
And anyway a sorry accident,
Though how are we to keep our streets in order,
And goods for shoppers safe and shoppers safe?

Billy Furr must have had a plan,
Flashing on out with a case of beer,
To streak back in to get another load
For sale, for use, for just the hold of it—

You know, the grab bag children sometimes have
For play at birthday parties roundly held
Each year for each of them.
I'm not reminded by what Billy did.

Perhaps it couldn't have been otherwise,
Though no one's sure just how the shot was fired.
It burst his chest just below the heart.
Life's pictures showed him running and then sprawled.

I know it fits that Billy Furr was killed.
We in America have a special dance
We do in harmony, like an assembly line.
Sweet Billy Furr got caught in it, that's all.

Poets are meant to draw a general rule
From things that seem to randomly exist. And I,
Not Billy's mother, who couldn't have been surprised,
Will wait for justice that will never come.

JOB SPEAKS TO GOD

It was my wife who asked, not me.
I like the others thought you would relent
once you had seen how my days were spent,
a blotter to your dose of misery.

It's part of the trap thinking leads you to
to have a first false premise prove the next one right.
I didn't mean the suffering to attach to you;
it travels in the world like crops and blight.

Why did you answer for it then and why
allow the Devil to turn into argument
that you select those who live and die?
What but your word can tell us what you meant?

The problem of having a talk with me
is that I have to lie to be believed.

EVOLUTION

Women in age
lose their gentleness,
men their appetite.
What once was met with joy
now stirs confusion,
and in late afternoons
old men dozing don't recall
how sleep came on.

The Wisdom of Prayer

I praise thee Lord because I won't
take the risk that if I don't
You, for your reasons darkly kept,
find natural the further keeping
of me and mine in further weeping.

I seek thee Lord because I fear
Your never being here or near
or anywhere that can be named
makes infinite the guiltless error
of men's lives lived in random terror.

I beg thee Lord to give a sign
that will give heart to me and mine
(all so easily beguiled)
to bear our pain until your mending,
to wake to heaven at life's ending.

BARGAIN

Comfortless as I am,
grieved though I may be,
I will not turn to prayer
for my infirmity.

God, if he's there at all,
and has a sway on things,
may give me credit for
my living silently;

especially if he notes
how great the clamor is
from those who still have hopes
their call to him will be
received appealingly.

I leave to them my place,
even if unearned,
to take it back again
once in Infinity.

THE IAMB SPEAKS

Would I exist
without the pause
the silent space
that makes the noise
between two thoughts
I may invoke
in my expected
usual stroke?
Or does my meaning come around
when I insert the empty sound
to echo what has just been said
and guess at what lies ahead?

Guess Whose Pantoum, Harold Bloom

Bleached to similar beige refulgence,
the river's stones assemble for next year's feast
intricate in the glower of the sun's bulb,
like gestures swaddled in a plural unity.

The river's stones assembled for next year's feast
stay at a distance limp
like gestures swaddled in a plural unity.
Of mourning night ended in another birth.

Stayed at a distance lumped,
the natives, soundless like the river's moons,
end night in the morning of another birth.
They undulate the passage from dismay.

The natives soundless like the river's moons
intone their blessings on the maidens stilled
through undulated passages and dismay.
Why then the sudden break

from blessed intonations made still
in the fierce air of remembrance?
Why then the sudden break
when all was hinged save the sunless white?

In the fierce air of remembrance
protrudes each fathomed memory,
all hinged save the sunless white,
each hinged, each draped, each furled.

Each fathomed memory protrudes
bleached to similar beige refulgence,
each hung, each draped, each furled
and intricate in the glower of the sun's bulb.

MESSAGE

Death died a rich man
and to his richer relatives
did conjugate his verb
and no one heard.

A Completed Description of the Truth

Snails seen and what they don't and mean
and worms alike from start to ending
where straight lines curve and not gets knotted
and the peek of stars is a snowflake long
what breath reveals of the glassblower's dream
if aligning causes gives results their cure
what ladder love uses when it wants to see
oh, that other color that I meant to paint
the hum of things that can't be fled
why's the first answer all questions need
and what a truth is, is what the truth is.

Riddle II

Much northern used, I have a southern name.
Held by my silence all my siblings speak.
Nothing is mouthed except as I am mute.
I most appear where mostly I am not
and stay in rhythm by remaining still.

God's imagers take to themselves my birth
by using me in bracing up their line.
But I'm the maker who out of nothing sets
the branch above from the branch below,
who makes the petal's edge, marks my lady's breath.

TRIOLET

Why can't the night keep dark as well
the places day keeps hidden from me?
It is in black that I can tell
how deep the falls that rise around me.
Entombed I am. None can dispel
the jagged darkness that surrounds me.
Why can't the night keep dark as well
the places day keeps hidden from me?

INSTRUCTIONS

You must read the manual with care
and note the various steps necessary
to be taken, in their proper order,
so that you can fully benefit
from your acquisition and not fail to qualify
for the bonuses declared from time to time.

First, you must take the time
to discover and to mark the necessary
modes, tones, and patterns, and in their proper order,
which are likely to qualify
you and your situation for the care
from which you wish to benefit.

Followed strictly, you will note the benefit
from your so marking, which is necessary
to the other's belief that you qualify,
and not just from time to time,
for attention, concern, and care
and all, of course, in their proper order.

All steps, followed and done in their proper order,
will enable you both to qualify
together and to profit from the benefit,
even if each thin deposit of time
thickens to make necessary
and stale sorrow and care.

There is no substitute for care,
and nothing here below, read now or at a later time
(constant readings will be a benefit

but always in their proper order),
will avoid for each of you the necessary
actions of those who may be lame to qualify.

Know that you both will do things that qualify
others, for whom you have boundless care,
to derive from your readings the benefit
(now obviously obtained in the proper order,
since nothing ever undertaken can alter time
thus no longer making precautions necessary)

of care and know that you have caused the necessary
events in time to benefit and qualify
others, by then always in their proper order.

BLOOD SUGAR

More times than once I may have had a thought
as polished, sane and airy—bright with ease
as any jeweled box the poet made.
He and his others in multitudes of times
have fashioned ecstasies no use can wear,
and, thinking, I can form them back to mind.

My doctor says my thoughts will jumble up
if there's too little sugar in my blood.
(He may have said too much—I can't be sure).
I saw it happen just the other day:
my thoughts like drunken steps did not proceed
until some counter-potion was added in.

Just sweeted blood and the right pond water
deliver the emerald frog on the mud shore.

STILL LIFE

Someone (is it the father?) leaning down
to the listening (is it stricken?) child looking up—
I don't want to hear the explanation,
or even know that it's taking place,
even if miles from here.

THOSE DAYS

Once, years after I was young
and braided stacks of lives
had come to intervene,
blurring what I could recall
though not enough to let the yearning out,
I passed a place where that young time was spent
and stopped and stayed to berth my memory.

I sought the spots decades don't change
to propel me back so I could exclaim
"Yes, it was here!"
and jar my memory back to present use.
Nothing came of it but a willingness to leave,
and leave the past in its scattered regrets.

I've often passed the anniversary of my death,
perhaps like you, mute and unthinking every time.
Will I know, when that Tuesday comes, to strain
against the blurring of its brother days?

GUBBINAL

The world is ugly,
And the people are sad.
—*Wallace Stevens,* "Gubbinal"

That wound,
the snagged beak's indifferent damp,
that flowering rot:
I know how it seems.
It's not what you think.

The calm in the torturer's hand,
that gape,
the vacant look of the broken cheek:
I know what you've seen,
it's not what you think.

That birth,
the breath that ebbs the more it's breathed,
that sorrow carved:
I know how it feels.
It's not what you think.

It's light fragments juggling.
It's heaves of seasons,
a cartwheel, an entertainment,
an interlude.

How to Keep from Being Devoured

The black shadow
that moves around your chair
in the room surrounded by dusk

may be your dog
looking for a comfort spot.

Don't look to verify,
assume you know.
It might turn into a leopard

and devour you
if you catch its eye.

Sonnet

How wise it was for whoever invented speech
to make no string of words able to reveal
the truth that hides in each of us for each.
Look how ably my explanations conceal
the breed and color of my true intent.
The truth that squirms and begs to be declared
needs more than words before it's shown and spent.
Yet it's not in silence that the truth is aired:
sounds corral meaning words cannot contain.
Long moan, slight sigh, and shriek are speeches made
that string whole lists of things no words can name.
The feel of feeling is not in words portrayed.

Still, if I were to touch your soft hand and cheek,
I would, like Herrick, be compelled to speak.

EXPLANATION

God must mean for us to reason
that the flower first in bloom,
taut and shining, is not altered
even in its dying season.
God's the present ever missing
till we meet it when we die.
Life's the ambush of tomorrow
and the sorrow of goodbye.

AUDIT

Up to now echoes are not
      the first thing said.
Up to now if I've called for help
      my rescuers haven't heard me.
Up to now the present is discernable
      only as past.
Up to now it's not clear
      what love entitles me to.
Up to now there is no real evidence
      that anyone's out to get me.
Up to now the misery of thin children
      happens in remote places.
Up to now I have lived no day as if
      it reduced my remaining days.
Up to now I've not looked around
      to see if I'm alone.
Up to now the death of one season
      starts another.
Up to now the poem I haven't written
      is as good as it will be when I write it.
Up to now moonlight has revealed
      nothing but continued expectation.
And up to now it always ends up raining.

NOTES

JANUARY 13: The title of this poem refers to the birthdate of the author's eldest daughter.

RIDDLE I: In a note to Phillis Levin, the author said this poem is "a sort of puzzle spoken by a poem that has experienced being made."

HART CRANE: The actual date of Hart Crane's death is April 27, 1932.

JACKSON, MISS., NOVEMBER 6, 1987: Ross Robert Barnett (1898-1987) served as Governor of Mississippi from 1960 to 1964; he was an advocate of racial segregation. In a note to Phillis Levin, the author said this poem "attempts to reflect the folly of learning nothing from experience." The full headline above Barnett's obituary in the *New York Times* read as follows: "Ross Barnett, Segregationist, Dies; Governor of Mississippi in 1960s."

THE KILLING OF BILLY FURR: This poem refers to the 1967 race riot in Newark, New Jersey, and to photographs of William Furr, who on July 15, 1967 was shot in the back by police as he fled, holding a pack of beer. The riot began the night of July 12 and ended on July 17; it was incited by the arrest and beating of a black taxi driver and the rumor that he had been killed. Furr, who lived in Montclair, had traveled to Newark to collect an unemployment check and look for another job; as the riot escalated the bus lines stopped running, and Furr was stranded. He and a friend entered a liquor store broken into the day before, took a case of beer, and were loading it into the trunk of his friend's car when a squad car pulled up. *Life* magazine reporter Dale Wittner and photographer Bud Lee, who had spoken with Furr earlier that day and met him again by chance only moments before the shooting, witnessed the police action that followed. Twenty-four-year-old Billy Furr was left to die on the street. Two of the pellets from the shotgun blast went by Furr and struck twelve-year-old Joe Bass Jr., who was seriously wounded. Wittner's article, "The killing of Billy Furr, caught in the act of looting beer," appeared with Lee's photographs in the magazine's July 28, 1967 issue; the cover photo showed Joe Bass lying unconscious on the asphalt in a pool of blood.

RIDDLE II: The speaker of this poem is a *caesura*, a pause or break in a line of verse.

About the Author

William (né Gérard) Louis-Dreyfus was born on June 21, 1932 in Ville-d'Avray, on the outskirts of Paris. His American-born mother and French father separated when he was a small child; both remarried. In October 1940, months after France fell under German occupation, his mother brought him and his sister to live in New York; his father fought in the Resistance and in 1943 joined the 1st Free French Division. At the end of the war his mother resettled in France with her two children, but several years later William returned to the United States to continue his education. He attended a military boarding school, where he was a member of the boxing team. He received his undergraduate degree in English literature from Duke University in 1954, a law degree from Duke University in 1957, and then worked in the litigation group at Dewey Ballantine in New York City until 1964, when he joined the Louis Dreyfus Corporation. From 1969 to 2006 he led the Louis Dreyfus Group, a privately held commodities-focused company founded by his great-grandfather, Léopold Louis-Dreyfus, in 1851. From 1998 to 2008, he served as President of the Poetry Society of America. In 2001, he completed an M.A. in creative writing from Antioch University McGregor. His poems have appeared in the *Hudson Review*, the *New Criterion*, *Plume*, and the *Southwest Review*; his translations from the French have been published in *AGNI* and *Boulevard*. William Louis-Dreyfus had a lifelong passion for poetry, art, and social justice. He died at his home in Mount Kisco, New York on September 16, 2016, a few days after completing this collection.

Printed in the USA
CPSIA information can be obtained
at www.ICGtesting.com
JSHW021957150824
68134JS00055B/2324

9 781597 098694